A LIFE WITHOUT LIMITS
Your Guide to a Life of Freedom

Zan Packard

LTA Publishing
San Francisco

ISBN-13:978-0615499192

LTA Publishing
San Francisco

~To my father ~
An elegant man who always
walked on the edge of wild.

ACKNOWLEDGEMENTS

So many steps and stages had to be completed for this book to happen. I had to break free from my self imposed prison and begin living the life I was meant to live: Free and loving and adventurous.

Even though I started out an exuberantly wild and carefree child whose only care in the world was what was around the next corner, I morphed into a fearful and unhappy little girl which continued into adulthood. The reasons *why* do not matter now. How I changed back and remembered who I used to be *does* matter.

I would like to acknowledge those who have seen that spark of the joyous little girl hiding deep inside my adult persona. They are the people who have loved me unconditionally – even when my joy and exuberance was hidden out of sight.

Everyone I have met on my journey has given me a precious gift. We've laughed together, loved together, lived together or fought together – I thank you for being part of my world.

CONTENTS

INTRODUCTION

"You were once wild here. Don't let them tame you."
Isadora Duncan

One day, idly flipping through the pages of a catalog, I came across a bracelet with the inscription: "You were once wild here. Don't let them tame you." On that day those words leapt off the page. I will never forget the emotional jolt I felt in my heart when I read those 10 seemingly simple words. That inner part of me that recognizes TRUTH yelled "Yeah!"

That same part of me also immediately remembered how wild and free I was as a young child – feeling that life was always an adventure filled with discovery waiting around every corner. At that tender age I never realized that there might be limits to life.

I sat there in a daze as I achingly remembered who I used to be – the *me* I came into this world to be – not the me that I had become.

I sat there feeling lost and trapped and stuck and even heart broken when I realized that I *had* let them tame me. That single moment was the first step into an inner journey to reconnect with my inner, joyous self; an adventurous spirit filled with love and light and passion for everything I haven't yet discovered.

This book is part of my own journey, but the steps that I have taken to get from stuck to free work for everyone. These days I encounter so many people who know they are stuck too, but don't know what to do about it. This book is for all of us.

Each one of us becomes stuck for different reasons – and usually for very good reasons at one time in our life. But this book is all about letting go of the things that no longer matter and no longer serve us.

Being stuck looks different to everyone. For me, I avoided trying new things. The unknown felt unsafe to my emotional well-being. This avoidance became a habit and I began to live life focused on playing it so safe that risk became intolerable.

You can see the vicious cycle that this behavior caused: the world is unpredictable and always changing so to be safe, I placed myself into a box that kept the world out – but it also kept me trapped inside – suffocating from my safeness.

In order to begin to live a life without limits, I had to learn to practice taking risks again. I had to learn to not only lean into fear, but to seek it and to embrace it.

By doing so, I didn't eliminate fear from my life . . .

I changed my
RELATIONSHIP
with it!

Fear became my hallmark telling me that I was on the right path: the path to freedom.

You might feel stuck because you've accepted a life by default: That's the life you just let happen because it's been handed to you by someone else. You have forgotten that you have a choice and a voice and you've accepted someone else's terms for your life.

This happens to most of us in many ways. We become busy and overwhelmed and we just take what is given to us because we lack the time, energy and commitment (and dare I say clarity?) to actively create a life worth living. If you don't know what matters most, you don't know what to choose and what to refuse – you just keep saying yes, more please!

But you know that something is missing from your life or you wouldn't be reading this book – you know that there is more to life than what you're currently living – and *you're right!*

This book is for all of us who know that life does not have to have limits. We can be wild, adventurous and expand into worlds we only faintly remember dreaming about. Life can and must be an adventure every day. This book is about remembering how.

Tell Me... What will You do with your one, wild, Adventurous Life?

HOW TO USE THIS BOOK

We each have a thinking brain and a feeling brain. Your subconscious is the intuitive part of your feeling brain where all your inner knowing originates. I call it your Inner Source. It holds all the answers to your life.

The conscious part of your brain is mostly ego-driven. Ego is self-centered and cannot get out of its own way. It cannot feel or dream; it can only react based on known information. It can easily lull you into thinking it has all the answers because it is so darned logical. But logic isn't all it's cracked up to be.

Inner Source can guide you with a greater clarity. It isn't constrained by logic and thus can dream and create and invent things you never knew existed.

Inner Source uses a particular voice to communicate with you, but you must first learn to recognize that voice. With recognition, you can then begin to trust the messages, and from there, you will learn to act on them.

Inner Source is already your best friend, but soon it will become your lifeblood. You won't want to do anything worth doing without checking in with your Inner Source.

The activities in this book will help you become better acquainted with your Inner Source. It is the path to a life without limits.

DAILY JOURNALING:

One of the best ways to get in touch with your Inner Source is to practice daily journal writing. There are many ways to do this, and I encourage you to try them all. Mix them up when you feel a bit stagnant. Here are a few that will get you started – but these are by no means the only ways to do your daily journaling.

Stream of Consciousness: For this method, you put your pen to paper and write whatever comes into your thoughts (do not stop to edit or understand your words). The goal is to get everything out of your thoughts and onto the paper without thinking – no judgment and no *figuring out what it means* while you're writing. You can figure things out later if it seems important.

This process allows for a couple of things to happen. One is that your Inner Source will begin to use this as a way to communicate with you. For some of you, your ability to hear your Inner Source may be a bit out of practice, but it's been waiting patiently for you to be ready to listen. With daily journal writing, Inner Source will soon get the idea that you are ready and open to communication.

The other benefit is that you can dump all those Ego-driven thoughts out on to the paper thus freeing up some mental space to think new thoughts in new ways – creatively.

Dear Diary: This is a method for you to go over the day's activities and find out what, if anything, is hanging around that needs to be addressed and released. If you find yourself writing about an event and you can still feel a strong emotion when you revisit it, then you can simply acknowledge the event/emotion and find a way to move on without dragging anything negative with you. As you will find, when we drag our emotional attachments

along with us, they have the potential to become limiting beliefs and behaviors – precisely what we are working to let go.

As you write in your journal about your day, pay attention to how you feel when you remember – the best time to let go is NOW, so this method will assist you in keeping clear of baggage.

Sentence Stems: One of my all time favorites – I always get a surprise when I do these – and yes, I use the same 20 or so over and over again and always get a different outcome. A sentence stem is a word or beginning of a sentence that you then journal. An example is: "Doorway"; or "If I could, I would…" You can make your own on index cards and just do a blind choice for the day's writing. The beauty of this method is that your mind always goes where you need to go to work through your stuff.

{
JOURNAL WRITING IS
SINGLE-HANDEDLY
THE
MOST IMPORTANT
PROCESS
OF ANY INNER GROWTH
AND RECONNECTION
TO INNER SOURCE.
}

Journal writing is the best way for you to really hear what your thoughts are saying – and if you hear something that doesn't sound right or doesn't make sense, you can then take the steps to change it. It's great, because it always keeps you in charge – remember a life without limits is all about intentional living which is all about having choices.

TIP: Putting your honest thoughts on paper is a daring, courageous move. After all, what if someone were to find it and read it? If you find yourself holding back – not really writing what's coming into your thoughts, then I suggest that you use a tablet or loose-leaf paper so that you can easily shred or burn it right after your journaling session. You see, it really doesn't matter that you keep your writings or even reread your writings. The work is in the initial transfer of your thoughts to the paper – it's been referred to as a 'brain dump' and I can't think of a better analogy because you are indeed dumping the thoughts from your brain onto the pages.

This helps you see your life more as an observer *and* it helps keep your thoughts clear. By letting go of all those thoughts and feelings you can then concentrate on listening....sweet, sweet listening. The Truth of your Inner Source will make your heart sing....all from a pen and paper and the willingness to do some inner work.

COURAGEOUS QUESTIONS
MUST BE ASKED ◇ ◇   ◇

Courageous questions are those questions that we often avoid in life – sometimes they are painful to think about, but often they are just too darned difficult to answer because our thinking brain gets in the way of the Truth. When we try to 'figure things out' we often become more confused than ever.

Here's the deal: You already hold the answers to all your questions about life. You just have to learn to ask the right questions to get to those answers.

The questions in this book are designed to get you moving on an inward journey toward your core being – your Inner Source. They are designed for you to answer your own questions – no one knows *you* like you do.

Change need not be difficult, but it must involve conscious thought and action. Through self-knowledge we become increasingly aware of the 4 W's of our behavior: What, When, Where and Why. With awareness comes the ability to choose. We can keep what works for us or let go of limiting behaviors and move into the life we were meant to live. But we need the truth to know what that life is.

These questions are based on the principle that we all have an inner guide, an Inner Source. Your Inner Source is communicating with you all the time – awake or asleep – but first you have to learn to listen and recognize your Inner Source's delivery.

.... When you answer any of the questions in the *Courageous Questions* section of each chapter and eventually work through the expanded questions at the back of the book, your answer will be exactly what you need to hear at any particular moment – that also means your answers could change each time you ask– it just depends on what your Inner Source wants you to know.

So don't think that just because you've already answered a question that you shouldn't answer it again – that is a great way to go deeper in stages – kinda like peeling an onion....each new answer is like a layer of your soul that is filled with new information.

NEVER stop asking questions – they are the juice of life. Here is your first question:

Tell me ~ what will you do with your one, wild, juicy, Adventurous Life?

The framework that you will use with these Courageous Questions involves guided writing techniques. The Questions themselves guide you down a path that will allow your Inner Source to take over and give you the information you need to let go and move forward.

It is recommended that you start each question with a short relaxation technique and invite your Inner Source to join you in order to move forward into your right life. Simply close your eyes, take some deep breaths and tell Source that you are ready to listen.

You can begin with the first question and move through all of them sequentially, or you may work with the one that speaks to you the strongest. Let this be a time where you are fully in touch with your higher self and go where spirit takes you. You might find it useful to stay with a question for a few days, or weeks. You are in charge. Let your inner guide lead you, and you will always be on the right path.

You will notice that some questions appear more than once. This is because those questions fit many categories. There are also several questions asking mostly the same thing, but stated in a different way....trust that you will hear what you need to hear to move you forward.

If a question comes up more than once and you'd like to move on, by all means do so. This is your journey and your life. If you answer these questions with as much depth and insight as you are capable of, right now, you will have all the answers you need to accomplish getting you back into the life you were meant to live.

1

RECONNECT TO YOUR INNER SOURCE

"Once you begin to get clear
about what really matters,
you can see where you are
stuck and that's when you can
start taking the steps to
let go."

This is where the fun begins – this is where your life changes from ho-hum and predictable to fun and exciting – this is when you begin to look at life as one big wonderful adventure.

THE CALL OF THE WILD:
THE MOST ASTOUNDING THINGS HAPPEN WHEN YOU LEARN TO LISTEN TO YOUR INNER SOURCE.

Call it Instincts, Higher Power, Inner Wisdom, God, Angels, Spirit Guides or Inner Source – it is the core of all that we are and is with us every step of the way.

We are bombarded daily with information and energy from others– so much so that many of us have lost touch with that special voice or *knowing* that helps us make choices for our higher good. Without this connection to Source our lives become a bit cloudier and less enjoyable; we feel uncertain, lost and somehow boxed into a life without purpose or joy.

Chances are you are reading this book because you're feeling that something is missing and that if you just had the right answer or technique you could find your path and finally feel like you're living again.

Rest assured your Inner Source is still there and probably still trying to communicate with you…In this book you will attain the tools to reconnect with this Source.

You will learn that you have been receiving valuable information from your Inner Source all your life and you will also learn to recognize this voice as your TRUTH. You will come to trust it above all else. And most importantly, you will easily be able to tell the difference between the voice of Inner Source and the incessant chatter of your Ego-driven thoughts.

Once you learn to invite your Inner Source into your conscious life you will be making decisions on purpose, not on reaction.

This is when you begin to make decisions and choices that are free spirited. You will find that things begin to flow. It is no guarantee that your life will be without challenges, but it is a promise that you can and will trust the information and guidance from Inner Source. There's a beautiful confidence that allows you to move forward without dragging your limits with you. Life becomes vibrant and free.

With this newfound freedom and trust in your guidance, you can better move forward to inspired action – no amount of knowing and preparing will make a speck of difference if you don't take action. Knowing is not the same as doing (duh)…when you're doing, you're fully living with intention. There are 4 critical steps to reconnect you with your Inner Source, so let's get started on them…..

STEP 1: INVITING SOURCE

When the intuitive muscle that is connected to our Inner Source is out of shape from disuse, we have to stretch it a bit to get it working properly again. Your Inner Source is probably sitting patiently in some quiet recess of your subconscious waiting for you to be ready and willing to listen.

I've discovered that the minute you invite this Source to your consciousness, it shows up – a more willing guest you will not find. The added bonus is this: if you continue to invite Inner Source into your life, (and you pay heed to its advice) the more it will show up without even being asked.

For now let's assume that your Inner Source is waiting patiently for you to be ready to listen. All you have to do is deliberately invite your Source to show up. It's that simple.

There are several ways to invite your Source to join you, but the best and by far the easiest is to just throw the invitation out there like this: close your eyes, take a few calm, relaxing breaths and say to yourself that you're ready to do some deep inner work in your journaling and would like your Inner Source to join you. You might also ask if there's anything you need to know right now.

My source has a bizarre sense of humor sometimes, and I love that. It keeps me from taking myself too seriously.

I've also learned that my Inner Source can scold me from time to time – however, I have grown to trust and love its advice so it now dispenses freely. If I sometimes get too much information or advice, I've learned to tell it to slow down a bit; I'm not ready to go down that road yet. Remember, you are always in charge and your Inner Source will always respect your needs.

Try this writing exercise:
Dear Source, Is there is anything that you'd like me to know right now? (Just write down whatever comes to you – DO NOT try to figure out what it means at this stage).

By talking to Source as if it were separate from your intellect (which it is), you are training yourself to listen differently. Your ego-driven thoughts might feel real, but they are often attached to your intellect and reasoning brain which functions based on past experiences – you want to listen to your higher wisdom – the voice that knows things your intellect doesn't know yet.

STEP 2: RECOGNIZING SOURCE

I'm sure you've heard the advice that you should listen to your intuition, but you've also probably wished that it would speak louder – or certainly in a language that you understand. How can we tell the difference between Inner Source and all the other pieces of information that bombard us daily?

That's the trick that this book will help you learn. By working a few simple steps, you will learn to recognize the voice of your Inner Source. Each chapter is designed to take your consciousness deeper and deeper, and at the same time allow your Source to come up closer and closer to your consciousness. By connecting the dots between your subconscious, Inner Source, and your consciousness you will learn to recognize not only your Inner Source, but your ego-driven thoughts as well.

Some people feel Source in their body. Some people have thoughts pop into their mind seemingly from out of nowhere and without explanation. Some people have dreams that give them important information. By learning to communicate with your Inner Source at will, you will become accustomed to the form of communication that it uses to 'speak' to you.

Are you paying attention to the messages that are currently being sent? It's different for everyone. I used to get vague hints that I needed to pay attention to something. Unfortunately they were so vague that I easily talked myself out of listening to them.

You can always tell when Inner Source has given you a message that at first you didn't understand because you find yourself saying things like "I knew this was going to happen", or "I shoulda listened to that voice telling me to go the other way". The goal is to not convince Inner Source to communicate more with you, the goal is to recognize and pay attention to the messages that are *already* being sent all the time. The more you listen and act on this information, the more you receive.

Remember, daily writing is a must. Your writing will alert your Inner Source that you are ready to listen. You may not recognize the information at first and it may be mixed in with a jumble of other thoughts that are fighting to be heard too. In this case, practice makes perfect – coupled with intention. Every time you sit down to write – in any method you choose, get in the habit of inviting Inner Source to join you. In time you will hear the messages as loudly and as clearly as a bell.

As you start to hear Inner Source, pay attention to how it comes to you. Is it a funny feeling? Do you hear a thought? Are most of your messages in dreams? Do you see things?

Think of all the times that you felt something before you actually knew it. That is your higher self at work – your Inner Source.

And the totally cool thing about your higher self is that the more you ask for guidance, the more help you get. But you have to ask.

STEP 3: TRUSTING SOURCE

You want the good news first? You have all the answers you'll ever need. You were born with all the answers, and you knew it too – way back then – you've just been trained to forget them. Let's change that.

Proving to yourself that Inner Source can be trusted is easy. Just take an imaginary train ride with me, and you will see that you have been getting plenty of messages from your Inner Source all along. You see, it's hard to take action without developing some level of trust, and that's what this next step is all about. You can prove to yourself that Inner Source is real, isn't hit or miss, and can be trusted.

All Aboard!

Please take a window seat and get comfortable – this is a necessary trip to help you remember that you have always received messages from your Inner Source. Rare is the person that hasn't had any – and if you're reading this book, I'm sure Inner Source actually guided you to buy it.

Your train is now slowly leaving the station. It is traveling at a speed that is just right for you to see and remember each event, but not so slowly as to get bogged down in the details of the events.

As you come to these events, I want you to notice how you knew ahead of time what was going to happen – even if only by a vague feeling. Did you feel it in your body (stomach clenched or headache)? Did you think a thought from out of the blue? Or see something that didn't seem right? Perhaps you had a dream that when looking back gave you big pieces of information that had you paid attention to, might have changed the outcome.

As your train travels back in time, you begin to experience an inner knowing about these events. You don't have to put words to it, but just notice the clarity with which you see.

Your train continues on and shows you more times when you might have had a funny feeling, a knowing feeling, and for whatever reason, you ignored the message. *Don't stop and dwell on any one event* – this isn't about how you should have listened, but instead a way for you to remember the messages that have been coming to you since the day you were born.

When your train comes to a stop, I want you to disembark and pick up your pen and journal. Quickly write down some of the key words that came to mind (remember that Inner Source is with you now, so trust the information you're getting).

Briefly write down as many events as you

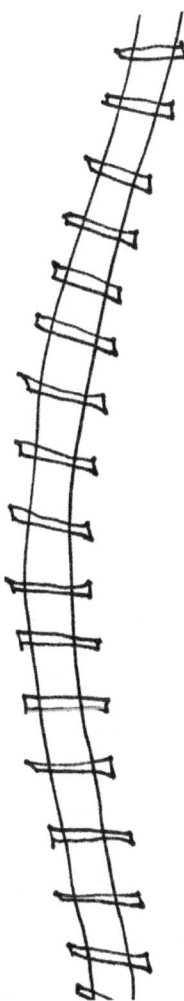

remember. Then go back and go deeper with one or two that stand out in your mind.

As you write in your journal, consider:

> ~ *How* Inner Source communicated,
> ~ *Where* you felt it in your body and,
> ~ *How accurate* was the information (in hindsight).
> ~ And . . . maybe just a smidge of the *process* you used in order to ignore it (so you know when you're doing it again).

As you do this with more and more events you will come to know that Inner Source has been with you all along, and will always be with you.

As you continue your journey to get to know Inner Source, you will be given much information that will help you choose your next steps. Inner Source will tell you exactly what limiting behaviors are holding you back.

Inner Source will tell you exactly what you can do to let go of them. Inner Source knows how big you can dream and is just waiting to show you an amazing new world. And, of course, the only thing left to do is to take inspired action – *on your terms.*

You have all the information you need for now and for always, but it will do you no good unless you take that first step. A ship, no matter how sound, cannot sail new worlds staying in the harbor. You are ready; let's get you a plan of action to move forward.

STEP 4: ACTING ON INSPIRATION

All the insight and information in the world will count for nothing if you don't take action. I can hear your concern right now. Whoa . . . action? You mean I have to *do* something? Yes, and not just do something, *change* something, and change isn't always easy. That's why doing all the steps in this book are important – it prepares you to change and enables you to find the support you need during the process.

Now that was the bad news first. The good news is this: small change can bring big results. Rarely does one have to toss everything out and start over (although many a wonderful new life started with being tossed upside down). When you are at the end of this book you will be seeing and doing the same things but from a different perspective – an expanded perspective that will allow you to feel very different about your everyday life. What's not to love about that?

If you ever feel like things are moving too fast, or that you are out of your depth, just slow yourself down. The only thing you have to keep in mind from this point forward is to ask yourself (with your Inner Source as guide) "What's my next step?" You can never go wrong taking things one step at a time. You are fully in charge and will always be, so relax and enjoy the journey.

COURAGEOUS QUESTIONS TO START YOUR JOURNEY:

What if you decided to create your future-self right now and align your energy with making that happen?

What if you could turn your vague feelings into crystal clarity and truly own what you already know?

What if you could discover the life that you were really meant to live, and developed the skills to achieve it?

2

LIMITATIONS, FEARS AND BLOCKS, OH MY!

WHAT YOU SHOULD KNOW ABOUT YOUR LIMITS:
Limits come in all shapes and sizes. The same limit can raise its ugly head in a variety of ways…always with the result of keeping you stuck. You know when you have limitations because you hold yourself back. You find yourself saying things like: "I wish I could…", or "If only things were different…" or "Too bad I'm not more…" these are all clues to some of your limits – actually they are the easiest ones to see and deal with, but it's also the best place to start.

Your thoughts usually accompany a longing or desire, but there is something in your belief system that prevents you from realizing your desires.

For every desire you shut down through a faulty belief you limit yourself - and enough limitations will get you stuck in life - can't move in any direction. When you are stuck, you aren't alive; you merely exist. Stay stuck long enough and your spirit dies a little - a slow painful death.

It's possible that you were guided to this book because you're so stuck that you don't know what to do. It's very likely that you know exactly what I'm talking about because I've just described 'you'.

The good news is that you are not alone. You may feel alone because you are only focusing on those who seem to have it all and seem to have the resources to do it all. WRONG. Even if someone has it all in one area, it's not uncommon for them to be missing something in another area.

Feeling like something is missing from life is so common it's like a sneeze. Everyone experiences it - sometimes the sneeze is from an allergy, sometimes it's because an unseen germ that has invaded our bodies, and sometimes a sneeze is just a sneeze.

Do not compare your life to your perception of someone else's life. We're all working through our own beloved 'stuff'. It seems to be the human condition. Perhaps if we didn't have any areas in which to become enlightened we wouldn't need to live in this reality. I can't wrap my brain around that concept, so I just accept that my 'stuff' is there to help me get the most out of my life.

I want to talk about that 4 letter "F" word: *FEAR*. It's a word that our society hates. We say things like "Never fear", or "Fake it 'til you make it", or "Don't worry, be happy." We don't like to admit that we have fears. We might have anxiety – or apprehension – or extreme caution, but we never admit to being afraid. We learned at a very young age that it's never O.K. to be a "Fraidy cat".

O.K. so I get that you don't want to even think about fear, but consider this: most of our limited beliefs are all about loss. We can't do *that* because we might lose our jobs, our health, our family, our self-respect, the respect of others. We have a real fear of these losses, and rightly so - our society doesn't make losing a fun proposition. We develop a fear of losing.

Consider also that almost every one of our limiting beliefs and behaviors can be narrowed down to a fear. There are 3 basic fears in life: Primal, Experiential and Ego-based. Knowing which fear you are dealing with is the first step in changing it – or more accurately changing your relationship with it. Fear will always be there – *how you react to it* can change.

Because I didn't understand the benefits of fear, I used to avoid it at all costs – which ultimately meant I avoided living at all costs. Now I find myself actively seeking it and actually walking into it – treating it as an adventure and loving the experience all the way. It is how I live my life without limits.

This book will help you change your relationship with fear too – it will help you understand, accept and appreciate fear.

FEAR IS NOT YOUR ENEMY:

Right now I'm sure it feels like your enemy but fear has so much to give you. It would be unwise and unrealistic to seek a life without fear. Instead it's better to seek a life where fear never stops you (unless it should). Imagine for a moment if you were not controlled by your fears (limitations) – what would you do? Where would you go? Who would you be? Pretty awesome isn't it? And highly possible.

I'll even go so far as to say that if you've been stuck for a while, you probably haven't flexed your creative dreaming muscles enough to really have a vision as to what is possible – don't worry, you will.

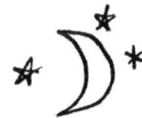

PRIMAL FEAR: this is the fear that alerts you to immediate danger. You really don't have to question it, you just know and you act – quickly – this is the fear that will save your life. This is the fear that you NEVER want to let go.

EXPERIENTIAL FEAR: this is a learned fear. Something hurtful in our past has happened and we learn to never do that again – also very helpful but where the trouble starts is when we globalize it – apply it to *all* similar situations.

Take a fear of dogs, for instance. If your neighbor's dog chased you and worse, bit you, you learned to be afraid of that dog – but you also might have learned to be afraid of all dogs. The kid in you, with your limited life experience, created a 'reality' where all dogs are dangerous. When you realize that a fear is experiential, you can choose to keep it or let it go – your choice, it ceases to be a knee-jerk reaction anymore.

I had unexplained insomnia from the time I was about 7 years old – there was no explaining event that anyone knew about, and the Dr. said it was rare for someone my age to have chronic insomnia. I just lived with it. I would have on-going nights of no sleep... and I actually enjoyed it – it seemed to give me energy (until the inevitable crash). I was 30 when I began seeing a hypnotherapist to help me stop smoking, and he uncovered something very interesting.

On the Patient Intake Form I checked the box indicating that I had insomnia, but then I declined treatment for it – the reason

I gave was "It makes me feel alive" (that is literally what I wrote on the form).

I didn't think anything of it when I wrote that, but it alerted the Dr. to an underlying event (and in my case a few events). You see when I was about 5 or 6 I had my tonsils out – and they 'put me to sleep' to perform the surgery. At around that time too, our family pet had an incurable disease and had to be 'put to sleep'. Of course, that meant she would never wake up once she went to sleep.

Well, my young, inexperienced brain equated sleep with dying, and I did everything I could to avoid it. When this was pointed out to me, I was stunned at how I had misinterpreted words that were originally meant to be kind and gentle into a recurring behavior that stayed with me for many, many years.

From that moment on, I've never had unexplained insomnia. It really made me consider the impact that words and events have on young minds and the rules that we create to explain our misperceptions.

We have all done this – how can a young mind with a limited world view do otherwise? I wasn't the type of child that discussed my thoughts with others, so I had the double whammy of creating my own reality without the help of mature thinking. I made my own rules . . . are you too living as an adult in a world of rules created by your child mind? Isn't it time to set some of them straight and let them go?

-☆-

EGO-BASED FEAR is a bit different: it's also experiential, but there's more Ego involved. Consider a time when you were very passionate about something; time when you were so caught up in the wonderfulness of an idea that it never dawned on you that others might not feel the same way.

You might have been shocked and hurt to learn that they disapproved or perhaps they laughed at your idea. You might have had that moment of delicious creative thought blown apart by someone else's negative reaction.

No one likes to be made fun of or teased. Depending on your personality, you might have shut down pretty quickly. You might have ultimately learned to never do *that* again – and add all those 'that's' together and you end up a person who has quit listening to Inner Source and instead become one who is listening to Ego: "Don't try new things, you'll get laughed at", "Don't make a mistake, others will call you dumb", "Don't get too far out of your comfort zone because you won't be able to make it back to solid ground", "Don't be *different*, it's just not safe."

When your Ego is in charge, it will keep you from risking. Ego has a very limited point of view and acts on perceived reality. It's the two year old in you that demands attention – loudly. The Ego stays in charge when you listen to it...but if you learn to pay attention to your higher wisdom (Inner Source), then your ego can be over ridden.

Of course no one wants to fail, or look silly, or be the brunt of ridicule– but we've all survived much worse. We have the skills to take it in stride – but if your Ego is still in charge then you haven't flexed your intuitive muscles in a while and taking back your life might seem too overwhelming.

It's hard sometimes to differentiate between your Ego and your Inner Source. However, remember that Inner Source is never nasty, mean or negative – it's always compassionate and helpful; it's always in your highest good. Your Inner Source can pop through at the oddest times (huh? where did that thought come from?), or comes to you only when you have quieted the incessant chatter of the Ego.

The voice of Ego, on the other hand, is usually yammering away non-stop, and often saying things that aren't very nice. Your Ego will try every trick in the book to keep you from listening to your Inner Source. It will discourage any risk because taking a risk is freedom, and freedom is not letting your Ego drive your actions. Ego isn't bad, it's just, well, ego: self centered and unwilling to look outside of itself.

Ego has a lot at stake and has been manipulating your beliefs and behaviors for many, many years. So it will take some effort – *conscious effort* - to disarm it.

Fear is typically the root of most of our limiting behaviors. It may visit you at the most surprising, unexpected times, but with the steps in this book you will never look at fear the same way again.......

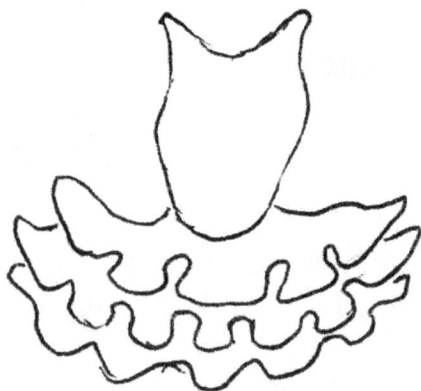

Imagine fear wearing a pink tutu:

(Go ahead, color it PINK)

Fear will no longer stop you because you know where it comes from and you know what to do about it when it shows up. In short, you will *change your relationship* with fear. You will have the ability to say *YES* to a life without limits. It's so worth the journey. Won't you join me........?

NOTA BENE: CHOOSE YOUR REGRETS:

During a time in my life when I was grappling with a difficult decision I didn't see a real answer until someone advised, "If you can't make a decision on what to do, choose your regrets". I've used this advice in all areas of my life. It's often said that in the final moments of our days our biggest regrets will be the things we didn't do, not the things we did do.

So I say to you, choose your regrets – look ahead to a life well lived, and consider that if you ignore what you want to do today, will you regret that decision in your final moments?

I don't know about you, but I don't want to leave life regretting missed chances and opportunities. When I am living a life without limits, I am regretting nothing, and that is exactly how it should be.

COURAGEOUS QUESTIONS FOR LETTING GO OF LIMITING BEHAVIORS:

› What is getting in my way of living the life I want and deserve?

› What needs to change?

› What drains me most or makes me tired?

› Is the thought I am having now taking me where I want to go?

› What part of my life am I refusing to see?

› How would my life be different without my limiting behaviors?

AM I READY TO LET GO OF MY LIMITING BEHAVIORS AND STEP INTO THE LIFE OF MY DREAMS?

3

FREE TO BE

WHAT DOES *FREEDOM* MEAN TO YOU? I talk a lot about freedom in this book. True, it is what matters most to me, but I think it matters to everyone, too. Freedom gives choices and allows for internal growth. But freedom is a concept that needs to be carefully defined by each individual.

We can all agree to the Webster's Dictionary definition: *"The power of self-determination attributed to the will; the quality of being independent of fate or necessity."* But it's very important to define it in our own terms, too.

Knowing what freedom means to you will help give you the clarity you need to build a life that matters. Just because something is free to me and gives me great value, doesn't mean that you will derive the same benefits from it – only the things that fall within your definition of freedom will do that for you.

Just as there are 3 kinds of fear, there are also 3 kinds of freedom. There is Perceived (the freedom you think you have or don't have), Environmental (physical) and Expansive freedom. All three are important to each of us by our own definition.

The trick is to know your definition of freedom. Could you feel free if the ability to move your body was taken away? Could you feel free if you were locked away in some prison? How free are you right now?

PERCEIVED FREEDOM is a freedom that is yours despite your circumstances. It comes from knowing who you are; knowing what matters most to you. It comes from being connected to your Inner Source; believing in *you* even when no one else does.

Perceived Freedom can never be taken away. It's the freedom to be who you are – it's the freedom that comes when you trust Inner Source.

If you've ever wondered how individuals survived horrific events like being prisoners of war, Holocaust survivors, or anyone who has lost the use of their body, yet never gave up hope, this is the freedom that kept them sane and focused on the future. This is the freedom that helped them to never give up – not completely.

Hopelessness is the number one symptom of depression. We lose hope when we lose our perceived freedom. It's essential to reconnect to ones Inner Source. That is the first step in regaining one's perceived freedom.

ENVIRONMENTAL FREEDOM depends on physical circumstances – to literally be able to come and go at will.

Environment matters; make no mistake about it. If you can't get around on your own, then environment matters. If you feel like a fish out of water, then environment matters. If you find yourself in the midst of toxic people, then environment matters.

Sometimes you can change your environment, but often you can't – or if you can, it's a long, long process. Don't discount your environment – there might be little you can do right now, but as you will soon see, you can focus on the other freedoms that are available to you.

EXPANSIVE FREEDOM is the freedom that literally opens up your heart because your barriers are removed. It is when you step into a new way of being; of living; of interacting with your world. It is one of the results of working the steps in this book.

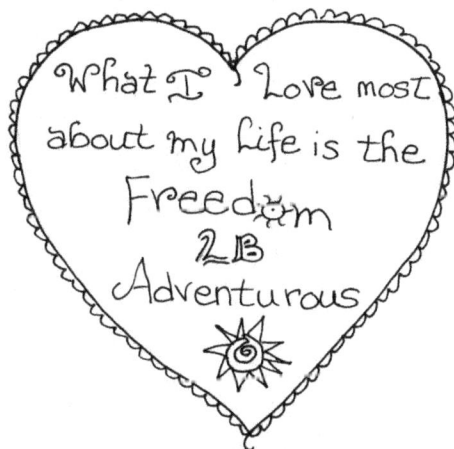

What I love most about my life is the Freedom 2B Adventurous

Several years ago I trapped myself by doing things I thought I *should* be doing instead of listening to my Inner Source. I was so busy achieving more that not once did I listen to my heart beg the question: *'What about me – when is it my turn?'*

At that time, my life was a series of tasks from my ever growing To-Do list, and I didn't know how to stop. Have you been there? So caught up in the life of your making that you don't even know which end is up anymore, you just know it isn't working? Something inside of me was screaming: *"Stop the world, I want to get off!"*

That's precisely when the Universe stepped in and handed me a back injury that left me bed-ridden for over six months and forced early retirement from my chosen career.

My world literally came crashing down around me. The months of recovery and rebuilding were slow and painful. I had to seriously reevaluate my entire life, yet ironically it was also the most hopeful I had felt in a long time.

My recovery gave me time to breathe, and time to identify the feelings that I came to know as my Core Values. Painfully, I realized that these were sorely missing in all areas of my life. I valued freedom and adventure above all else, and I had created just the opposite.

I had successfully stuffed my dreams down so far that I couldn't even recognize them. I kept them hidden away, stomped into submission in order to be what I thought I 'should' be.

There was no way I could decipher what mattered most to me in that state of mind. It was like total mental chaos.

I wanted a fresh start. I wanted a do-over, and I got just what I was asking for. Yet far from ruining me, the circumstances of my injury took me to new heights.

I started to feel alive again, because I started listening to what my heart was saying. I actively sought anything that made me feel free and adventurous because that's where my juice was.

What does your heart sing when no one else is around? How does it feel when you listen?

My spirit would soar when I was in the exciting moments of adventure ~ It would expand limitlessly when I just let go and trusted, and a simple, deep breath would feel like the world was bursting open inside of me.

However, adventure was just a part of my newfound joy. The other was the realization that I was reconnected to what matters most to me…to feel the wonder and joy of being back in touch with my Inner Source.

It's amazing the things that happen when we stay in the feelings that matter most. Do you know what your Core Values are? If you don't, then it's time to discover them…

Knowing the Core Values of who you are, and standing in your Truth will give you the ability to go where you've never gone before. It will give you the ability to see what's possible. It will change you at a cellular level.

You will be different and it will be like seeing the world for the first time. So if all of this sounds good to you, you're ready to roll up your sleeves and do some work. Let's begin.

COURAGEOUS QUESTIONS TO GAIN CLARITY

Conscious living means possessing clarity as to who you are today, while also understanding who you are meant to be. Conscious living is being mindful and making deliberate choices.

With clarity we can respond to our environment. We can choose what to make important and what to let go. Take charge of your life right now. Open up to your inner guide and see what is possible for you.

"Without Clarity we become reactive rather than proactive or responsive"

~What would my life look like if I lived in alignment with my core values?

~What do I use to avoid feelings?

~What are my emotions telling me?

~What is holding me back?

~Am I ready for change?

~When am I the most aligned with my inner Source?

WHAT IS GETTING IN

THE WAY

OF

MY CLARITY?

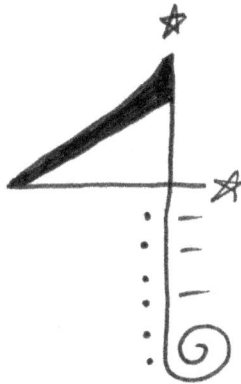

WHAT MATTERS MOST?

Do you ever wonder why some things affect you more than others? Why some sentiments bring tears to your eyes while others are merely interesting or perhaps not important in the slightest to you? It's probably because a core value is activated. A core value is the one thing, above all else, that you hold important. It is your deal maker or breaker.

You are way ahead of the game if you know what your core values are. Do you know yours?

What really makes your heart soar?

What makes you want to annihilate your enemies?

What matters most to you?

Not the things that your intellect says should matter – but the things that you're willing to risk it all for, to be willing to buck the tide because, to you, it's that important.

If you don't know what matters most it might be like being adrift on the ocean with no navigation – how do you know which direction to go to reach your place in the world?

It's important to identify your core values because everyone's are different. If you don't know yours, you will feel that something is missing from your life but you won't have the faintest idea what it is.

How do you know what to fight for if you don't know what matters? You might follow along on someone else's core values because they sound pretty good to you, but you can't take someone else's journey with them until you know it's your journey, too.

When you know your core values, you begin to seek out those values in everything you do, and your world feels much more meaningful and you're more engaged in living. But if you aren't living in your core values you might battle unhappiness, or the overall feeling that nothing is working in your life. And you know what? It isn't – not for you.

Once you identify your core values, don't align yourself with anything that goes against them – there is no right or wrong, there is only good fit or bad fit. I want you to set yourself up for success and you will never know how to achieve that until you discover your bottom line.

What do you stand for?

To figure out what your Core Values are, go over the list on the next page and circle the ones that seem to speak to you. It doesn't matter how many you circled, but I want you to go back and narrow it down to no more that 3 values. Don't worry about these being 'right' – you should do this several different times until you know for sure the top 2 or 3 that remain constant every single day of your life.

When you get three narrowed down, spend some time journaling on each word – that 's all the information I'll give you right now....just write the word down, and continue with whatever comes to mind.

Go on to the next word until you've journaled on all of them. Revisit this activity every other day for a while – it's very important for you to identify what matters most before you go much further. Your core values are your *platform* to begin creating a life without limits.

CORE VALUES LIST

Love	Gratitude	Honor
Courage	Commitment	Honesty
Adventure	Limitlessness	Spirituality
Empowerment	Independence	Creativity
Self expression	Beauty	Trust
Vitality	Authenticity	Merit
Security	Fairness	Respect
Diversity	Leadership	Responsibility
Duty	Learning	Responsiveness
Education	Leisure	Democracy
Involvement	Rehabilitation	Determination

CORE VALUES LIST

Joy	Reliability	Discipline
Justice	Resourcefulness	Humor
Discovery	Knowledge	Equality
Love-concern	Rule of law	Excellence
Loyalty	Safety	Experience
Meaning	Results-oriented	Productivity
Efficiency	Love-romance	Risk-taking
Empowerment	Love-care	Rootedness
Satisfying others	Expression	Union
Expression	Creation	Romance
Truth	Leniency	Care

It's easy to figure out what your Core Values are using this chart, and armed with this information you can begin to see what and where your barriers are. We all have barriers, but the ones that conflict with our core values are the ones that are keeping you stuck and holding you back.

I have a fear of horses (experiential), but I could care less because that fear is not keeping me from embarking on any desired adventures or pursuing any personal dreams. I won't waste my time fretting over this fear. It's understandable . . . it just is . . . and it's not getting in the way of the life I was born to live.

My fear of flying was another story (again, experiential). I had a lot of work to do on this fear because I wanted a life free to travel and explore new places. I had to deal with this fear before I could go any further.

True, I had to get creative to counter this fear, but in time I understood my limiting beliefs and devised a plan that would allow me to see the world – adventure on my terms. I still have a moment of anxiety when I book a flight, and I still have to go into my 'zone' upon take-off, but gone are the days when I refuse to fly. That wasn't a fear I had the luxury to keep if I wanted to get unstuck.

PUTTING MORE VALUE INTO EVERY SINGLE DAY:

So now you know what matters most to you because you've identified your highest Core Values, but let's explore where they are and are not in your life right now.

Hopefully you've spent some time with what each core value means to you – which is the first step – but can you also identify what things you do every day that fit within that core value? And even more importantly, what you might be doing every day that firmly goes against a core value? In the exercise on page 73 list some of your daily activities.

Try to get all of them (continue in your journal if you run out of room), from most important to mundane. Then spend a moment visualizing each activity – put a check mark in the appropriate column of + (adds value) or – (subtracts value). You should get a pretty good visual representation of how much of your day is spent in your core value and how much is working against them.

ARE *YOU* LIVING YOUR CORE VALUES?

Daily Activity	+	–
1- Make Phone calls		√
2- Walk the beach	√	
3- Write next chapter	√	

I set my Heart free

And it came back
to me ....

This is a really good time to take a break from reading and write
your thoughts and insights into your journal – just what did
you discover about your core values?

COURAGEOUS QUESTIONS TO HELP YOU DISCOVER WHAT MATTERS MOST

What activity is robbing me the most of my core values?

What can I do this week to add more value to my day?

What can I let go of that I don't really need to be doing?

If I were living strictly in my core values what would I be doing?

How have I withheld myself from life?

What am I unwilling to risk?

What is the decision that I have been avoiding?

WHEN WILL YOU TAKE YOUR NEXT STEP TOWARD YOUR HIGHEST GOALS?

Right now, just begin to get a sense of what your life could look like – if you don't know what's possible, you might not try for it. Don't worry about dreaming – it's always flexible and often changing.

Just because you want it today, as you evolve, so will your dreams…just get in the habit of flexing your creative muscle and dream big!!

Flex
Your Dream
Muscles

WHAT'S HOLDING YOU BACK?

You've done a lot of work up to this point. You now know what matters most in your life. So let's look at what's holding you back and keeping you stuck from a life that matters.

Your next step is to really look at your belief system. It is in charge of all that you do. By now, you're getting better acquainted with your Inner Source through your daily journal writing, and you probably have a sense of what is really stopping you from stepping into the life of your dreams.

The good news is that is doesn't matter if you start big or small when it comes to barriers. Usually the biggest step by far is simply recognizing them. When your barriers are out in the open they begin to change on their own.

For barriers to work at controlling you they need to remain hidden – once out in the open they have less power over you. By recognizing them you can choose to hang on to them or let go of them. Sometimes a simple acknowledgement is the most powerful: "There is (belief) that is holding me back – I choose to let it go".

Sometimes there might be lots of work needed on deep-rooted beliefs because they're buried under layers of other limiting beliefs. These become your 'onion', and you have to peel every blasted layer back, sometimes crying and sometimes fighting to get that last thin piece off once and for all.

But the first step is to recognize the behavioral patterns that you use to deal with life.

Do you say 'no' first without even considering yes?

Do you hang on to the known (even if it's painful) because it's familiar and you think familiar is better/easier than the unknown?

Do you stop yourself because you think you need more preparation – maybe schooling, experience or you-name-it?

Do you *settle* for an O.K. relationship (or worse) instead of asking for the one you really want – the one that feeds your soul and treats you with respect?

Do you feel less-than and not enough?

All of these are beliefs which create behaviors that will keep us grounded in our status-quo (in other words, stuck). Stuck in a world that just happened to us because somewhere along the way we forgot we could choose.

How to know when you are guided by your Inner Source – your Higher Good:

It feels all warm and cozy inside; your energy kicks up a notch or two; you KNOW it's the Truth – you may not be able to put it into words yet – but you *KNOW* it none-the-less.

It feels good. You want to throw your arms open to accept all the goodness of the Universe coming to you, because *this is it – really it,* you are on your way!!

….and then the Ego realizes that you are about to take action…and you come crashing down. "What are you doing?" you lament, "Who do you think you are?" scoffing at your plans, "Are you crazy?" demands a voice from within.

KNOW YOUR TRIGGERS:

Here's what happens when I listen to my Inner Source and decide to take action – my Ego will let me get into the planning stage for just about anything – we're safe there, my ego and I – but just let me start to take action and here's how it unfolds:

I get an inspiration – and it feels *so right* – so perfect – so exciting. I just KNOW that it's what I'm meant to do next. I take that first exciting, adventurous step in the direction of my heart....I move forward and get so excited. "Wow, this is it, I'm finally gonna do it!".

Then I crash into a wall, or fall into a deep dark hole and struggle to find my way. "What was I thinking?" "Who do I think I am?" become the words I hear more clearly than my Inner Source.

Yikes! I must be CRAZY

CHECK ALL THAT APPLY:

☐ What are you doing?

☐ Are you Crazy?

☐ who do you think You are?

☐ you can't do THAT!

☐ you'll Just fail

☐ you'll Just get hurt if You try

☐ It's too scary

☐ It's Never been done before.

☐ No one will believe You

☐ you don't have Time

☐ Quit Dreaming

☐ you're not ready

☐ why do you want to do THAT?

☐ Not Now

☐ why do You want to be Different?

☐ You have REAL work to do.

Once ego is done with you, you question your Inner Source and reaffirm an old belief:

{Belief}

"I am flighty". "I can't be taken seriously". "I'm not good enough to do this". "I can't even trust my own feelings". "I'm not enough and I need more". (Hear the despair and hopelessness? Notice how Ego can tromp on your dreams and beat you to smithereens? Notice how *loudly* Ego is yelling at you?)

(Truth)

When you take a step toward listening to your heart — your Inner Source — your Ego will play every trick in the book to stop you. Ego wants you to stay put — be stuck — and it will go to any lengths to keep you there because Ego does not know how to dream.

EGO WILL <u>NOT</u> LET YOU GO WITHOUT A FIGHT.

Ah Ha!

But I'm so much more aware of how my ego gets in my way. Now, when I crash into that wall or fall into that deep dark hole, I know it means that *I am on the right track* – if my Ego is uncomfortable then that is good. If my Ego feels threatened enough to throw the book at me then I must be on to something worthwhile.

From now on, when I hit that moment of fear and self-doubt, I will see it as a sign that I am doing EXACTLY what I need to be doing to follow my heart!

And that is good news, my friend –
Very good news indeed!

Even if I can't let go of a limiting behavior right way, I can at least identify the triggering event: what caused the knee-jerk reaction that is getting in my way.

What do you seem to do automatically when faced with certain circumstances? What behaviors do you wish you could change? Do you become too shy? Pay attention to *when* that happens. Are you a basket of nerves? *When* does that happen? What events trigger those feelings? Knowing a bit more about that will help you anticipate the barriers even before they get triggered – or at least recognize that you're dealing with a trigger which may, in fact, have little reality on the current situation. It makes all the difference in the world to note to yourself 'oh, there's that reaction/feeling again'. It allows you to notice, acknowledge, and let go.

Know your triggers and you can have a strategy for when they are activated. Fear won't go away completely, nor should it. But you don't have to let it control your behaviors. You can take charge and make choices based on current circumstances, not knee-jerk reactions.

In your journal begin to take note of the behaviors that are getting in your way. If you have insight into them, definitely write it out, but for now, just start to notice where you are blocked from moving forward.

COURAGEOUS QUESTIONS TO GET UNSTUCK

The things that are stopping me are…

Where am I focusing my energy right now?

What can I do to shift my energy to where I want it to go?

What am I resisting or refusing to see?

Where do I limit myself?

When am I most free?

If I Were Unstuck What Would I Be Doing Right Now?

What would your life look like if you were unstuck?

6

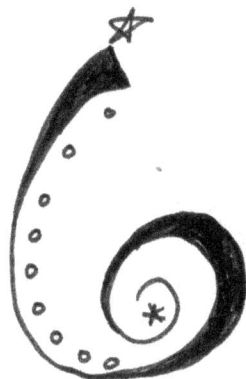

INSPIRED ACTION

All the money in the world does you no good unless you are willing to spend it. You have a wealth of knowledge within you; it's now time to invest in yourself by taking action. But it's probably going to feel a little unfamiliar to you at first. You've been stuck for so long that inaction feels normal (suffocating, but normal). So spread your wings gently at first.

Give yourself the gift of going slowly and building your confidence. Just taking that first step to decide to take that first step will seem momentous to some of you – I know it did for me, because I knew in my very core that there was no turning back.

Like Pandora's Box, once released there is no going back...but unlike Pandora's Box being released is the best thing that could possibly happen to you. Have fun with your first steps for they lead to new worlds.

THE KEY to moving forward is to do some magic wand thinking. Spend some time in your dreams. You know which Core Value means the most to you. You know which activities allow you to be in that Core Value.

Now, take your magic wand and wave it over your journal and begin dreaming of the most amazing life you could possibly imagine.

You have no limitations – money is no object, time or education or age or social status is no object. What would you be doing if you knew you couldn't fail? What does your heart dream about?

It's safe to unleash these dreams because you can trust Inner Source to guide you to your highest good. Just because you dream it doesn't mean that you have to do it. It's just dreaming and dreaming activates creativity. Creativity activates Inner Source (or vice versa, I'm never sure which).

A life without limits means that you can go or do anything you want to do – you know this in your very core. BUT remember, just because you *can* do it doesn't mean that you will or that you should.

I often think that is why we shut down our dreaming along the way to adulthood – we can 'feel' the power in each dream and it feels so real that we confuse that feeling with the necessity to act. Imagine how chaotic life would be if we followed every single dream. To keep us safe, our ego-driven thoughts put the brakes on dreaming too much…just in case.

The truth is, you will gain more energy each day if you entertain the 'what ifs' about life. What if you won the lottery? What if you could go on that world class trip to Alaska? What if you couldn't fail?

Since you now know your Core Values, you know what feelings are the most important in your life. When you consider the 'what if life' when you dream about possibilities, you can seek to find the same feelings in your everyday living with no major changes, just some simple shifts in attitude.

If feeling helpful is one of your highest values, what can you do today, *right now* to be helpful? You don't necessarily have to quit your job and trek to Africa to work in an orphanage – but you do need to add more activities that give you that feeling of being helpful.

If connection is one of your highest values, what can you do today to make a connection? Your neighbor, the clerk at the grocery store or a stranger walking down the street; connecting is really about listening and validating someone. We all need that – so go make a connection with someone. You don't have to go back to school to learn to be a counselor – you can embrace the Core Values that mean so much to you in many, many ways.

I love to move to new locations – I've been doing it straight out of high school. In fact it was part of all my daydreams as a child. I dreamt of living in Europe, South America, all over the United States… It's something that I'm born to do – there is no good or bad to it, it is just a part of me that I accept and love.

Even though I move a lot, I have loving long-term relationships. I've simply learned how to say no to things that limit my sense of freedom and choose friends that allow me to come and go at will.

Dr. Seuss said it best:

"THOSE THAT MATTER DON'T MIND AND THOSE THAT MIND DON'T MATTER."

I've embraced that philosophy for many years now.

I also begin to feel trapped when I accumulate too much stuff so keeping my possessions to a minimum feeds my Core Value of *freedom*. With minimal possessions I feel that I can move at a moments notice.

The reality however, is that I can't. There are always too many other factors involved. I can move, but it still takes planning and strategic execution. That's reality, but my *feelings* are that I travel as light as what works for me. It isn't so much about doing; it's much more about how we feel about what we're doing. The specifics don't matter as much as the feelings attached to the action.

THAT is where attention must be paid. Know what matters, and you will know what you can do. Know what you can do and you will know what barriers you have to let go. Inner Source will guide you through all of your life if you will let it. It's time to listen up, and start living the life you were meant to live – A Life without Limits.

Loving the Adventure

COURAGEOUS QUESTIONS TO INSPIRE ACTION:

The courageous questions here are designed to inspire you to dream bigger than you have since the time you were little and you believed anything was possible. These questions will help you get back to yourself...to get you moving on your own true path...to get you to believe again.

Are you ready to step into a world without limits? A life filled with passion and purpose; a life so rich in rewards that you feel free and adventurous in everything that you do?

What am I meant to be?

What have I settled for?

What would life without limits look like?

What would life without limits feel like?

What support do I need?

Where am I too comfortable?

Where do I limit myself?

What is my Truth?

Isn't it time you started living the life you were meant to live? Life filled with passion and adventure? Life that brings joy to everything and everyone around you? To be free, wild, untamed and always moving forward? Isn't it time to have . . .

A Life Without Limits?

7

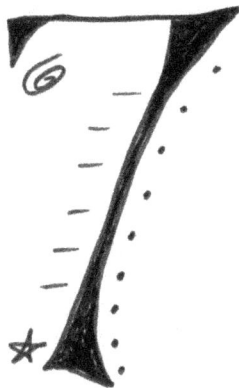

AUTOMATIC
SELF-NURTURING MODE

You've done a lot of work letting go of limiting behaviors. You're stepping up and taking inspired action to create the life of your dreams. It's time to fill up your bag of tricks for when those nasty ego-driven thoughts come a calling – and they will, rest assured.

It's time to develop some automatic self nurturing strategies that will become activated at just the right time: BEFORE you get into reaction mode.

Here are a few things that might help:

"YET"...
The word *yet* has the most amazing power. Whenever your ego-driven thoughts start bashing you and telling you what you aren't or what you can't do – get in the habit of deliberately adding the word 'yet' to the end.

It seems to take all the negative focus out of the diatribe. Try it: "You're not smart enough – yet", "You're not good enough – yet", "You're not O.K. – yet." See how it makes a negative seem less harsh?

Whether the statement is true or not – the word 'yet' implies that it's not permanent; that you can change it at some point in the future. It makes it feel so much less hopeless – so much less awful.

"WHAT WOULD MY BEST FRIEND SAY?"...
This is another exercise that is designed to get you treating yourself like your best friend – the friend that is all about how

wonderful you are and who wants to support you in everything you do.

You probably have a real-life best friend so you can insert their name in the sentence, but if you haven't learned how to attract people who are your real allies and support you with unconditional love (yet), then do a journaling exercise that creates the most supportive person you can imagine and let that person have a voice to help you counter-balance mean ol' narrow-minded ego when it's trying to knock you down a peg or two.

Even if you have a best friend that would go to the ends of the earth for you – it's always a good idea to develop a friendship with yourself too . . . again, only you know what really matters at any given time.

"AH, THERE IT IS AGAIN. . ."
Truer words cannot be spoken when your ego-driven thoughts arrive. Simply acknowledging them goes a long way to diffusing them. Seeing the thoughts for what they are – an attempt to

keep you from growing – will take the sting out of their words and empower you to let them go.

THINGS I'M GRATEFUL FOR. . .

It's nearly impossible to focus on the negative when you begin to list the things you're grateful to have in your life. And I do mean list – as in paper and pencil. A journal just for writing the things you're grateful for is fun and can always be revisited in moments of need. The next time your ego wants to jerk you around, just jump into gratitude mode and that nasty voice will all but disappear.

YOUR LUSCIOUS BAG OF TRICKS....

Start right now by listing things that you can do with little time and money, since those are often very real limiting factors. Things like lighting a candle – putting certain music on – taking a nice hot bath or long shower – trying on your favorite pair of shoes – you get the idea. When you are tired and your defenses are down even summoning up some gratitude might seem too much effort. That's the time to step back and do something to break the negative energy that is holding you hostage.

Post that list somewhere to remind yourself how quick and easy it is to shift your attention.

MAKE A VISION BOARD. . .

This is such a fun project. Just gather a stack of old magazines and start going through them. Cut out any words or pictures that speak to you.

Once you have a pile of cut-outs, go through them again, and see if they can be grouped together into some meaning or category. You can vision on any one thing or a variety of things that are of the most importance to you.

I usually do a vision board every January and post it on my refrigerator where I see it often so I'm constantly reminded of my dreams. I divide my board up into quadrants with an image or picture that represents me in the center.

I typically focus on career, environment (a new place to live?), travel and social life. The photos and words always seem to have the perfect place on my board and it is always a soothing thing to visit when my self-doubts come calling.

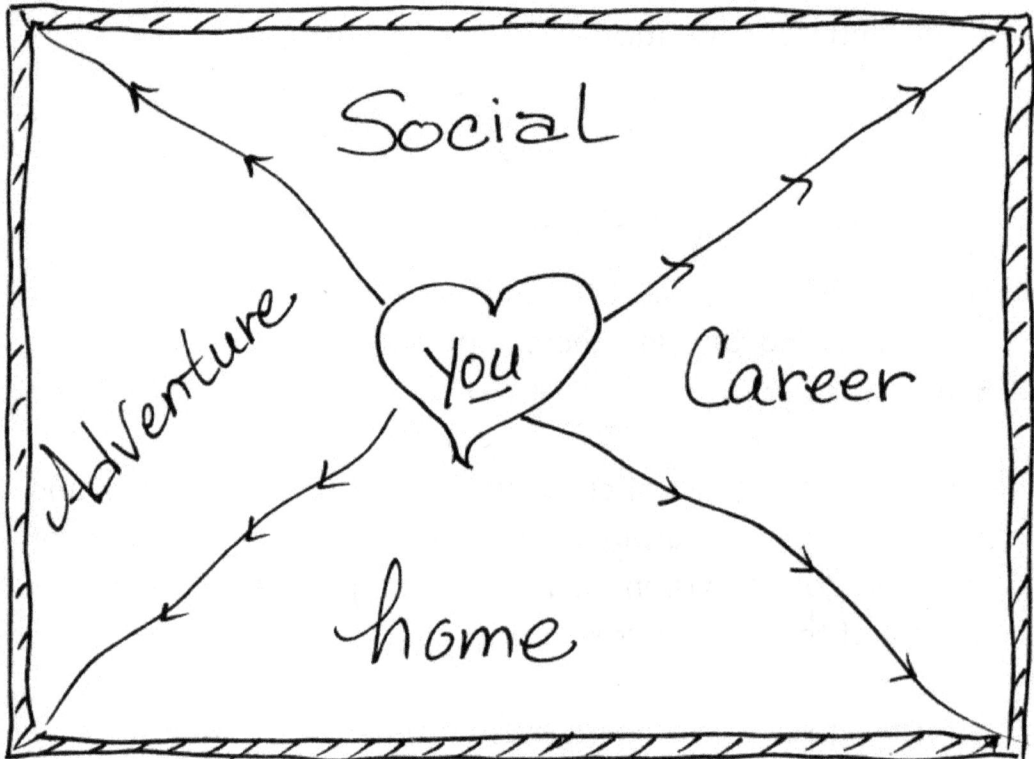

Social

Adventure

you

Career

home

Vision Board

AND . . . REMEMBER TO LAUGH.

Laugh.

Out Loud.

Often...

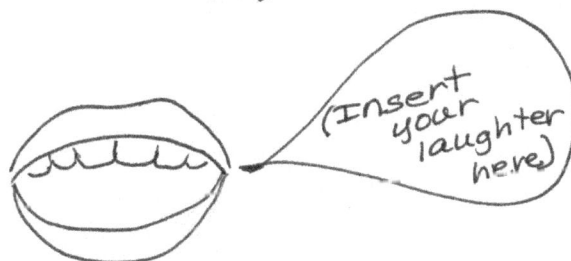

(Insert your laughter here)

IF NOT NOW, WHEN?

If you have done the exercises in this book then you are well on your way to reconnecting with your Inner Source and designing a life of your dreams – and if you haven't taken that first step yet – well….you certainly know what that step is by now.

I realize that letting go seems like a loss at times, but it's not possible to have *more* without making room for something new.

View your life like a closet that has been accumulating 'stuff' for years. If your closet is too full, then you cannot put another new thing in there no matter how wonderful it is – and so it is with your mind.

Releasing thoughts and behaviors is just a process needed to make room for new – and Ego-be-Damned, new is always good. *New* keeps us on our toes and feeling alive.

I would like to think that everyone will find their dreams and bring their visions into reality. It's true, you know, you are always creating your future by what you think and do today.

Use the guided writing techniques you've learned from these pages. Write everyday. You will be amazed by how deeply you will come to feel about your writing.

Readers who have never really written anything in their life tell me how hooked on the process they've become.

So I repeat the question:

"If Not Now, When?"

APPENDIX

COURAGEOUS QUESTIONS

The framework that you will use with these Courageous Questions involves guided writing techniques. Writing down your answers to each question will allow your inner voice to be heard.

This is your voice that knows who you were meant to be and if you listen, will guide you toward clarity, purpose and the ability to create your future-self.

It is recommended that you start each question with a short relaxation technique and invite your Inner Source to tell you what you need to know in order to move forward into your right life.

You can begin with the first question and move through all of them sequentially. Or you may work with the one that speaks to you the strongest. Let this be a time where you are fully in touch with your Inner Source, and go where spirit takes you. You might find it useful to stay with a question for a few days

or weeks. You are in charge. Let your inner guide lead you and you will always be on the right path.

You will notice that some questions appear more than once. This is because those questions fit many categories. There are also several questions asking mostly the same thing, but asked in a different way....trust that you will hear what you need to hear to move you forward. If a question comes up more than once and you'd like to move on, by all means do so.

This is your journey and your life. If you answer these questions with as much depth and insight as you are capable of, right now, you will have all the answers you need to accomplish your greatest desires...your premium dream.

Are you ready to find out the answers to your questions?

Are you willing to spend time with the answers that come to you?

It's your life, isn't it time you started living it your way?

COURAGEOUS QUESTIONS FOR CONNECTING TO YOUR INNER SOURCE

"You cannot go forward while looking back. Hindsight is not your friend, it is your teacher.

Intuition is your friend – learn to listen, trust and act on it."

We've all had those funny feelings that, in hindsight, we wish would have caught our attention. Life could be so much richer, fuller, and easier if we learn to recognize those funny feelings as messages from our inner guides.

So the first step to developing your intuition is to ask the questions that put you in touch with this part of your Inner Source. The next step is to learn to trust what the message is, and the final step is to learn to act on it.

1 When do I ignore the messages from my inner guides?

2 When I get a funny feeling, where do I feel it in my body?

3 When is my intuition at its highest?

4 What needs to happen in order for me to recognize my inner voice?

5 Where am I not willing to go, that I need to go?

6 What am I being right about?

7 When was the last time I recognized my inner voice as my inner guide?

8 How can I listen better?

9 What do I need to know about developing my intuitive ability?

10 What is it to be intuitive?

What is your intuition telling you right now?

COURAGEOUS QUESTIONS FOR LETTING GO OF LIMITING BEHAVIORS

Limiting behaviors typically develop as protective mechanisms. As humans we are always trying to explain our world. Depending on a variety of circumstances, our explanations developed (rightly or wrongly) from a very young, immature world view.

> *"Much of who we are today is based on experiences that happened when we were very young."*

If you ever find yourself reacting in a way that you don't understand, it's highly likely that your behaviors have been triggered from some explanation you constructed as a child. Do you know an adult who had a hissy fit and everyone said was acting like a two-year old (hopefully not you). Well, they probably were – their behavior was constructed at the age of two, and they never released it.

It's not hard to see that our behaviors, while deeply ingrained, can truly hold us back until we indentify them and release them. These questions are designed to help you see what behaviors you want to keep and what behaviors you want to let go.

1   What are my strengths?

2   What is getting in my way of living the life I want and deserve?

3   What positive changes am I making in my life today?

4   What needs to change for me to move into the life I was meant to live?

5   What holds my energy back?

6   What drains me or makes me tired?

7   Is the thought I am now thinking taking me where I want to go?

8 If not, what thought would?

9 What part of my life am I refusing to see?

10 What behaviors do I need to let go?

11 How would my life be different without my limiting behaviors?

12 Where is my energy going? What can I do to shift my energy to go where I want it to go?

13 Who says you can or can't?

14 Whose shadow am I living in?

15 What is most important to me?

16 What do I need to let go?

17 If you had it to do over again, what would you do?

18 What is your main obstacle?

19 What concerns you the most?

COURAGEOUS QUESTIONS FOR GAINING CLARITY

Conscious living means having the clarity of knowing who you are today, and who you are meant to be.

> *"Without clarity we become reactive rather than proactive or responsive"*

Conscious living is being mindful and making deliberate choices. With clarity we can respond to our environment. We can choose what to make important and what to let go. Take charge of your life right now. Open up to your inner guide and see what is possible for you.

As you begin to ask these Courageous Questions you may want to revisit some or all of these questions several times. Think of your life as an onion with multiple layers. The more you peel away, the closer you get to the core. It is the core that holds your truth. With exquisite clarity comes the ability to t stand in your truth. Choose wisely. . .

1   What is it to live in alignment with your core values?

2   What are my expectations?

3   What do I use to avoid feelings?

4   What is integrity?

5   If your life depended on action, what would you do?

6   What are the possibilities?

7   What are your emotions telling you?

8   What are you choosing, right now?

9   What do you need to know, right now?

10 Whose approval are you seeking?

11 What or who allows your energy to soar?

12 What or who restricts your energy?

13 What is holding you back?

14 What needs to change to move into the life you were meant to live?

15 Are you ready for change?

16 What needs to happen to take your next step?

17 When are you most aligned with your higher power?

18 What are your strengths?

19 What are you most grateful for?

20 What is my higher good?

What is getting in the way
of my clarity?

COURAGEOUS QUESTIONS TO DISCOVER WHAT MATTERS MOST

If you don't know where you are going, how will you know when you get there? Goal setting is one of the most powerful tools for change. It brings together clarity, purpose and passion.

1   Who am I mean to be?

2   What do I need to know to get there?

3   Where do I want to be in 3 months, 6 months, a year, 5 years?

4   What are my core values?

5   What is possible?

6   What are your next steps?

7   What are some of the dreams you had as a child?

8   What is it like to have a full, rich life?

9   What is the difference between a wish and a goal?

10 Where is my attention, right now?

11 What do I need in order to reach my goals?

12 What is it to be creative?

13 What is it to be focused?

14 How have I withheld myself from life?

15 What is it to be passionate?

16 What is my soul's purpose?

17 When will I begin to take charge of my life?

18 Why not you?

19 What is out of alignment?

20 What am I unwilling to risk?

21 Is what I'm doing right now in alignment with my goals?

22 How can I have this be easy?

23 What is the decision that I have been avoiding?

24 What have I wanted to do and haven't?

25 What is completion? Where am I incomplete?

26 What did it take to get here?

27 What will keep me on track?

When will you take your next step toward your highest goals?

COURAGEOUS QUESTIONS FOR GETTING UNSTUCK

If you are feeling stuck in any part of your life, identify the area as much as you can, given your particular circumstances, then lightly hold that thought in your mind while you ask for guidance and answers from your Inner Source.

"These questions are designed to get you moving through some issues that you may not even know about."

Just be aware of what is coming to you....hold no judgment for a moment and just let the thoughts flow from your subconscious to your paper. Trust the process. Begin with these questions:

1 Where am I focusing my energy, right now?

2 What can I do to shift my energy to where I want it to go?

3 What am I meant to do?

4 Who am I meant to be?

5 What is possible?

6 What is the answer that is not clear yet?

7 What do I need to know?

8 What am I resisting or refusing to see?

9 If I were at my best, what would I be doing right now?

10 What is out of alignment?

11 Where do I limit myself?

12 What am I the most afraid of?

13 What am I hiding from myself?

If I were unstuck, what would I be doing right now?

COURAGEOUS QUESTIONS FOR INSPIRED ACTION

Maybe you've followed the rules all your life. Or maybe you've bucked the norms. But if you're not able to say that you are living your dream life, a life without limits and that you are soaring, then you might have been settling for your bargain dream. You know, the one that seemed the easiest to you? . . . The one that required less risk? . . . The one that just dropped in your lap? . . . And you just may have achieved a fair amount of success in your present life. But if it's not your *Premium Dream*, then you've settled for your bargain dream.

The Courageous Questions in this section are designed to inspire you to dream bigger than you have since you were little and you believed anything was possible. These questions are here to get you back to yourself...to get you moving on your true path...to get you to believe in your *Premium Dream*.

1   What have I settled for?

2   What am I here to accomplish?

3   What is my heart's desire?

4   Who am I meant to be?

5   What would life without limits look like?

6   What would life without limits feel like?

7   How will you know if you are on the right path to your Premium Dream?

8   What will it take to get there?

9   What support will I need?

10 What do I need to do next?

11 What am I most grateful for?

12 What can I do to my physical environment to have it nurture/empower me?

13 Where am I too comfortable?

14 What is it to be exceptional?

15 Where do I limit myself?

16 What is it to be passionate?

17 What am I building?

18 Do my dreams align with my core values?

19 Who am I becoming?

20 What is my truth?

New Book Coming Soon:

Come Play With Me

*Inspiration for Finding Fun & Adventure
Around Every Corner*

Be sure to also subscribe to:
Loving the Adventure Blog

Discover the online place where Zan shares her insights, her
challenges and all her newly found, adventures. Zan interacts
joyously with her readers, and as a subscriber, you will also be
informed of any workshops, book signings, and new releases she
has in the works. Zan can be reached though her website
www.LovingtheAdventure.com

Here's wishing you many adventures of your choosing and a life well lived.

Loving the Adventure

Zan Packard is passionate about adventure, playing, and loving life. She has lived all over California and currently calls San Francisco her home. When not writing or sketching, Zan spends most of her days ferreting out adventure in everything she does. This is her dream and she is truly living A Life Without Limits.

Notes – Sketches – Dreams

Notes – Sketches – Dreams

Notes – Sketches – Dreams

Notes – Sketches – Dreams

Notes – Sketches – Dreams

Notes – Sketches – Dreams